P9-EER-644

JOSEPH PULITZER

JOSEPH PULITZER

HISTORIC NEWSPAPER PUBLISHER

by **Martin Gitlin**

Content Consultant:
Daniel W. Pfaff, Professor Emeritus of Journalism
Penn State University, University Park, Pennsylvania

ABDO
Publishing Company

CREDITS

Published by ABDO Publishing Company, 8000 West 78th Street, Edina, Minnesota 55439. Copyright © 2010 by Abdo Consulting Group, Inc. International copyrights reserved in all countries. No part of this book may be reproduced in any form without written permission from the publisher. The Essential Library™ is a trademark and logo of ABDO Publishing Company.

Printed in the United States.

 PRINTED ON RECYCLED PAPER

Editor: Erika Wittekind
Copy Editor: Paula Lewis
Interior Design and Production: Emily Love
Cover Design: Emily Love

Library of Congress Cataloging-in-Publication Data
Gitlin, Marty.
  Joseph Pulitzer : historic newspaper publisher / by Martin Gitlin.
      p. cm. — (Publishing pioneers)
  Includes bibliographical references and index.
  ISBN 978-1-60453-765-9
  1. Pulitzer, Joseph, 1847–1911—Juvenile literature. 2. Journalists—United States—Biography—Juvenile literature. 3. Publishers and publishing—United States—Biography—Juvenile literature. 4. Newspaper publishing—United States—History—19th century—Juvenile literature. 5. Newspaper publishing—United States—History—20th century—Juvenile literature. I. Title.

  PN4874.P8G58 2009
  070.92—dc22
  [B]
                          2009009994

TABLE OF CONTENTS

The Union Army of the Potomac marching through Washington DC in 1865

BIRTH OF A JOURNALIST

The last bullet had been fired. A sweet silence finally fell over the land. After four years of fighting, the bloodiest conflict ever fought on U.S. soil was finally over in April 1865. But the stench of dead bodies permeated its towns and countryside.

The Civil War had officially ended, and the United States was united again.

Joseph Pulitzer was among the soldiers riding with a Union Army regiment in a victory parade in Washington DC. Pulitzer was far from the celebrated figure he would eventually become. He looked and felt out of place as the people cheered the battle-worn heroes who had saved the nation. The Hungarian immigrant had barely arrived on the shores of his new country in time to participate in the struggle. The thought of achieving battle glory, with which he had been so preoccupied as a young teenager, no longer excited him. With the war over, he moved to New York City and began looking for work.

He was not alone in his search. Thousands of other war veterans joined him in the borough of Manhattan. There, the contrast between rich and poor was striking. In a district called Five Points, some veterans picked up odd jobs while others were relegated to begging for money. Just a few blocks away, on and around Wall Street, wealthy people lived, worked, and shopped.

With limited English and unfamiliarity with his new country, the 18-year-old Pulitzer struggled

Rags to Riches

While in New York City following the Civil War, the down-and-out Pulitzer sometimes went into the fancy French's Hotel for a shoe shine. He had only his army uniform for clothing, and it had become worn and tattered. A porter believed the presence of such a raggedy outfit would offend the rich visitors and asked Pulitzer to leave the hotel. Twenty-three years later, on his forty-first birthday, Pulitzer bought the hotel for $630,000. He had it demolished. He replaced it with the tallest building in the country— a $2 million skyscraper that became home to his newspaper offices.

to find work, much less start a career. So he traveled to New Bedford, Massachusetts, to seek out employment on a whaling ship. Unfortunately, the whaling business had suffered from Confederate cruisers during the war and had yet to recover. Pulitzer applied for a job, but the ship's captain turned him down.

Soon, he was back in New York and still searching for work. Despite his fine education, his thick Hungarian accent and poor grasp of the English language was not appealing to potential employers. Jobless and homeless, Pulitzer shuffled about the streets of New York in his raggedy army uniform. At night, he was forced to sleep on benches and in wagons parked on cobblestone streets. But he was not about to snooze outside when the cold winds began to blow in autumn 1865. He sold his only belonging—a silk handkerchief—for 75 cents to buy food. Then he sneaked onto a train heading

New York City in the 1880s

to St. Louis as a stowaway. He stumbled off the train hungry, cold, and flat broke. Pulitzer was also discouraged to learn that he had to somehow find a way across the Mississippi River to reach his destination.

Starting Fresh

Fortune, however, smiled upon Pulitzer that rainy day. He asked the deckhands of a nearby ferry if he could ride the boat across the river from East St. Louis to St. Louis for free. They informed him that if he could shovel coal into the fire in the boiler room, he would not only travel for free but would even be paid. Pulitzer later said,

> In my condition I was willing to say anything and do anything. [The engineer] put a shovel in my hand and told me to throw some coal on the fire. I opened the fire box door and a blast of fiery hot air struck me in the face. At the same time a blast of cold driven rain struck me in the back. I was roasting in front and freezing in the back. But I stuck to the job and shoveled coal as hard as I could.[1]

After a disagreement with the ferryboat captain, Pulitzer found his way to St. Louis. He had earned enough working on the ferry to rent a room. He immediately started looking for a job in his new city. The city's *Westliche Post* was a German paper he could easily read and understand. He was soon in the library poring over want ads in the newspaper. In the following months, he toiled at several poorly paid, dead-end jobs. He had thought of St. Louis as a paradise when he arrived in that midwestern town, but it was treating him no better than New York City. Life went from bad to worse when he paid five dollars to a con artist who promised him and 40 others work on a sugar plantation in Louisiana. He and his fellow victims boarded a steamboat that was supposed to take them to that job, but instead it dropped them off in the middle of nowhere. The group trudged back approximately 40 miles (64 km) to St. Louis, vowing revenge on the crook every step of the way.

Little did the 18-year-old Pulitzer know that his latest misery would open the door to one of the most brilliant and successful publishing careers in U.S. history. Pulitzer wrote about the scam and submitted his story to the *Westliche Post*. The publication ran the story. Part owner and coeditor Emil Preetorius was impressed with Pulitzer. He provided the young man with a few writing assignments.

GAINING CONFIDENCE

That work did not lead Pulitzer immediately to a journalism career.

Odd Job

Pulitzer certainly was not picky about accepting jobs when he first arrived in St. Louis. In one job, he worked at an army barracks and received free meals, but his job was as caretaker for 16 mules! He found the food inedible and the mules too difficult to control. Two days after arriving on the job, he quit.

But his determined and confident approach to writing piqued the interest of others in the office building that housed the *Post*, particularly physician Joseph Nash McDowell and attorneys William Patrick and Charles Philip Johnson. McDowell secured a job for Pulitzer keeping records of the 3,527 victims of an 1866 cholera epidemic. When that work ended, Patrick and Johnson suggested he work for the Atlantic and Pacific Railroad as a land-grabber. This job required him to secure permission from counties to allow the railroad to pass through.

The attorneys were impressed with Pulitzer. When Pulitzer finished his work for the railroad, Patrick and Johnson encouraged him to pursue a law career. They even cleared out space in their office for Pulitzer to study and gave him free access to their library. While studying for his law degree in 1867, Pulitzer also took time to officially become a U.S. citizen.

Pulitzer proved remarkably sharp, passing his bar exam in 1868 and

Déjà Vu

During his short stint as a notary public, Pulitzer was visited by the ferryboat captain who had hired him to stoke the boiler when he arrived in East St. Louis. The man needed some documents sealed, but when he recognized Pulitzer, he was far from thrilled.

"He stopped short as if he had seen a ghost and said, 'Say, ain't you the . . . cuss that I fired off my boat?'" Pulitzer recalled. "I told him yes, I was. He was the most surprised man I ever saw, but after he had sworn himself hoarse he faced the facts and gave me his business."[2]

becoming a notary public. Still, he was not swamped with clients. Folks were not interested in giving their business to a 21-year-old with little experience and broken English.

Westliche Post coeditor Carl Schurz came to his rescue. Impressed with all that Pulitzer had achieved in such a short time, he offered the Hungarian immigrant a job as a reporter. Pushing his law career aside, Pulitzer accepted the position with tremendous enthusiasm. "I could not believe it," he recalled years later. "I, the unknown, the luckless, almost a

Near-death Experience

The job Pulitzer landed with the railroad company was fraught with danger. The railroad company was just beginning and needed permission to build on the land. Pulitzer's job required him to travel throughout the wild Ozark territory on his horse to obtain such permission. He did not work alone. Pulitzer had an aide.

Tragedy struck one day as Pulitzer and his aide rode in those wide-open spaces. The two men attempted to cross the flooded Gasconade River on horseback but were swept up in the current. The aide and his horse drowned. Only Pulitzer's talents as a swimmer saved him. He managed to reach the bank and pull himself from the river.

A nearby farmer, who had watched the scene unfold, greeted the drenched Pulitzer. The elderly man invited Pulitzer into his farmhouse and offered him whisky, chewing tobacco, and pipe tobacco, all of which Pulitzer declined. The farmer told Pulitzer jokingly that he would never make it in America if he did not drink, chew, and smoke.

After the incident, Pulitzer began work on what would eventually become the Atlantic and Pacific Railroad.

boy of the streets, selected for such responsibility—it all seemed like a dream."[3]

Indeed, it was a dream come true for the young man whose life had been a nightmare since he arrived in the United States. But there would be both sweet dreams and nightmares on the horizon.

A painting of Joseph Pulitzer, circa 1885

Mako, Hungary, the birthplace of Joseph Pulitzer

In Hungary, Hungry to Fight

*P*ulitzer was not accustomed to the poverty
that gripped him from the moment he
stepped foot onto the shores of the United States.
He had been provided a life of wealth and culture as
a child in Hungary. On April 10, 1847, Joseph was

born to Philip and Louise Pulitzer. The family was of Magyar descent. The couple lived in the town of Mako in southeast Hungary, near the Romanian border. Brother Albert was born four years after Joseph, followed by their sister, Irma.

Joseph's father was a grain dealer who had a successful business. In 1853, the business closed. Philip Pulitzer had earned enough money that he could retire. He moved the family to Budapest, the country's capital. Joseph was a sickly child. He was educated at private schools and at home by a tutor his parents had hired. A curious child, Joseph immersed himself in his studies. He mastered the German and French languages taught to him by his tutors. The Pulitzer family enjoyed the benefits of their wealth and were well educated and cultured. Joseph was particularly fond of theater, literature, and classical music. His dreams, however, had little to do with reading books or listening to his favorite composers. Joseph yearned to be a soldier and hungered for battle glory.

Birth Order

Joseph was not the first child of Philip and Louise Pulitzer as they set out to start a family in Hungary. He was, however, the first to survive. Louise gave birth to a son in the mid-1840s, but the boy, named Louis, died young.

DREAMING OF GLORY

But by the time Joseph was 11 years old, his father died of heart disease. A few years later, his mother married Max Blau, a businessman.

Story of the Magyars

The Magyar culture from which Joseph Pulitzer descended can be traced back hundreds of years. By the fifth century, the Ugric and Turkish peoples had joined into a single group: the Magyars. The group lived in what is now known as Siberia. They started moving south, and by the late ninth century, the Magyars settled in Hungary. The name "Magyar" translates to "Hungarian" in English.

The Magyars were powerful and overtook the Slavs and Huns living in the area. Magyar warriors invaded other areas of Europe as well, including Moravia in 906 CE. They became the dominant ethnic group of Hungary and remain the overwhelming presence in that nation to this day.

Magyars now use the term Magyar to distinguish themselves as the Hungarian-speaking group in that country as opposed to those who speak other languages, such as German or Romanian.

Approximately 9 to 10 million Magyars reside in Hungary. With approximately 2 million Magyars, Romania has the second-largest population base. The United States boasts approximately 1.5 million people with Magyar ancestry.

As a teenager, Joseph grew to be tall and lanky. He was approximately 6 feet 3 inches (1.9 m) tall and extremely thin and frail. He had a large, hooked nose and poor eyesight that required strong glasses. His unusual appearance made him a target of taunts from boys in the neighborhood, as did his excitable personality and critical nature.

FEELING REJECTED

In 1864, Joseph made his first attempt to join the military. That year, he tried to enlist in the Austrian Army but was rejected for his weak eyesight and skinny frame. Undaunted, he traveled to Paris in an attempt to join the French Foreign Legion, which needed men to serve in Mexico. But he was declined enlistment again—they did not need the young Hungarian.

Joseph refused to give up. He moved on to England and volunteered to serve with the British forces in their colonies in India. Turned down yet again, he stopped in Hamburg, Germany, on his way home. Joseph would not reach his destination. In Hamburg, his fortunes changed.

The Union Army had turned to overseas candidates for recruits to fight in the American Civil War. U.S. President Abraham Lincoln had attempted to draft thousands of men in the United States, but with little success.

Recruiting Trouble

As the American Civil War progressed, President Abraham Lincoln had little luck finding recruits for the Union Army in New York City. A number of poor Irish immigrants were drafted, but they did not necessarily care about the war. During the summer of 1863, many of them rioted at the prospect of enlisting. Rioters burned down buildings and were violent. Union soldiers were brought in to quell the violence. By the time it was over, hundreds had been killed.

Chess Skills

One particular skill that young Joseph learned would serve him well as he grew into adulthood. He developed into an accomplished chess player. It became a hobby that he continued to pursue the rest of his life.

The 17-year-old Joseph met one of the Union recruiters in Hamburg in 1864. By assuring the agent that he could ride a horse and shoot a gun, he managed to join the Union Army to fight in the Civil War. The agent arranged for Joseph to take a ship to Boston. Pulitzer was eager to arrive and determined to keep the enlistment money for himself rather than have it placed in the hands of the recruiting agent. So, he leaped overboard and swam through the water of Boston Harbor to shore. He then hopped on a train to New York City, where he was given $300 for enlisting.

Finally, Joseph Pulitzer would be a soldier. It certainly was not his skill as a soldier that would make him one of the most prominent Americans of that century and beyond. In fact, his brief experience in the Union Army made him wish he had never put on a uniform.

This U.S. postage stamp was created to commemorate the one hundredth anniversary of the birth of Joseph Pulitzer.

Union soldiers during the American Civil War

First Taunted, Then Embraced

The dream of being in the military finally had become a reality for Joseph Pulitzer. Undoubtedly with pride, he slipped on the uniform of a soldier and prepared to distinguish himself in battle. But he was to be terribly disappointed.

The most significant fighting Pulitzer did was with his own sergeant.

Pulitzer reported to his regiment at Remount Camp, Pleasant Valley, Maryland, on November 12, 1864. His problems began immediately. Upon meeting Pulitzer, the captain of the regiment yelled, "I don't want him in my company!"[1] Pulitzer's unusual appearance and limited English certainly did not endear him to his fellow recruits and commanding officer. The captain's response set the stage for the young soldier's experience. The other soldiers tormented Pulitzer unmercifully for his nose and for his poor English—even though most of them were German and spoke their native language, which Pulitzer spoke fluently.

Others made fun of his last name, joking that "Pull-it-sir" gave them an invitation to pull his nose. The repeated taunts drove Pulitzer to assault an officer on one occasion. Pulitzer punched a sergeant in the face. The violent act might have earned Pulitzer a court martial, but another officer who admired his talent as a chess player spared him.

Pulitzer played virtually no role in the Civil War. He took part in minor battles against Confederate soldiers, rode horseback, and carried a weapon but saw little action. As it turned out, his mold-breaking tendencies were more suited to a different career.

A Whole New Outlook

Pulitzer's earlier yearnings to fight on the battlefields had faded away. He set off for St. Louis, where he toiled away in low-paying jobs until getting his first break in journalism. He excitedly accepted a job as a reporter with the *Westliche Post* in 1868. He had no time for thinking about the past—or just about anything else. He threw himself into his work, toiling day and night. He shuffled about the streets of St. Louis and shook off the taunts from those who called him names such as "Joey the Jew."[2]

Many were impressed with Pulitzer's talent and aggressiveness. Emil Preetorius and Carl Schurz ran the *Westliche Post* and placed him on the prestigious beat of covering politics in the Missouri capital of Jefferson City. Pulitzer proved particularly adept at recognizing shady, corrupt politicians and bringing them to the attention of the public.

Though he made many enemies in the process, he also earned powerful admirers. Among them was Missouri Lieutenant Governor Henry Brockmeyer, who exclaimed,

An 1884 political cartoon shows Whitelaw Reid, Charles Dana, and Joseph Pulitzer. All three were journalists who were active in the movement to reform the Republican Party.

They think because he trundles about with himself a big cobnose and bullfrog eyes that he has no sense; but I tell you he possesses greater [speaking] ability than all of them put together. Mark me, he is now engaged in the making of a greater man than Editor Preetorius, or even Schurz.[3]

In 1868, Schurz became the first German-born citizen to be elected to the U.S. Senate. Pulitzer

Greeley for President

Pulitzer served as a secretary at the 1872 national convention of the Liberal Republican Party in Cincinnati, Ohio. Thereafter, he set out to campaign for presidential candidate Horace Greeley, who had been the most famous journalist in the country. Pulitzer's many speeches in Missouri and Indiana on behalf of Greeley—or the support of the Democratic Party—did not succeed in getting the candidate elected president. Little did Pulitzer and other Greeley supporters know that the candidate was in no condition to serve as president. Greeley, who lost to incumbent Ulysses S. Grant, was going through a mental breakdown and died in a mental institution within a month of losing the election.

would soon follow in Schurz's footsteps and become a politician. He showed up as a reporter to a Republican Party meeting in December 1869 and departed as its candidate for state representative. A representative had resigned his post, so a special election was needed to find a replacement. Pulitzer was not the first choice, but he won the nomination. Opponent Democrat Samuel Grantham was favored to win easily. Pulitzer campaigned with the same zeal with which he undertook his job as a reporter. Grantham, however, seemed destined to win the election, which was scheduled for December 21.

Pulitzer surprised everyone by winning handily—209 to 147. Though the 22-year-old was legally underage for the position, nobody noticed or spoke out. He soon grew a moustache and beard that made him appear older and more distinguished.

And he continued to work tirelessly, not just as a politician but also as a reporter.

Now Pulitzer could expose corruption from both inside and outside the realm of politics. There was enough dirty dealing in the Missouri legislature to make Pulitzer quite unpopular. He was tormented for his idealism, his sense of duty, and his crusade for honesty in politics.

TROUBLE WITH HIS TEMPER

Among Pulitzer's targets was Edward Augustine, a building contractor who was willing to pay the county court judges to approve the construction of a mental hospital. He would have received several hundred thousand dollars to build it. But Pulitzer introduced a bill in the Missouri Senate that would abolish the county court, whose five members had made a habit of unfairly favoring friends, and he used his job at the *Post* to support it. As a result, Augustine and Pulitzer had a confrontation at the Schmidt Hotel.

The specifics of the scuffle that followed have been debated. Some

Social Life

By his mid-twenties, Pulitzer was giving more thought to his social life. Upon becoming coeditor and majority owner of the *Westliche Post*, he moved into the Lindell Hotel, which was popular with bachelors. Fellow bachelors praised him for his outgoing nature and even his penchant for practical jokes. Pulitzer also relaxed on occasion by going horseback riding.

contend that the tough, burly Augustine attacked
Pulitzer with a gun. Others say the contractor was
unarmed. In either case, Pulitzer shot Augustine
in the leg, below the knee. Pulitzer stood trial for
attempted murder and was found guilty, but he
received only a $400 fine. But not all was lost for
the young representative. The bill he had proposed
passed, which limited the influence of the court.
In addition, Augustine lost the contract for the
mental hospital. Shortly thereafter, in March 1870,
Pulitzer's term as Missouri representative ended.

But Pulitzer's time in public office would
continue in a new position. He accepted an offer
from Missouri's governor to be one of three police
commissioners in St. Louis. Pulitzer also joined
Carl Schurz's movement to do away with corruption
in the Republican Party and oppose the reelection
of Republican President Ulysses S. Grant. Always a
dedicated worker, Pulitzer gave 60 speeches—mostly
in Indiana and Missouri—to promote his cause. But
his work did not succeed. Grant was reelected in
1872. Frustrated, Pulitzer changed political parties
and became a Democrat.

The failure to reform the Republican Party
was not entirely negative for Pulitzer. Schurz

and Preetorius thought the loss would result in diminished readership and sold Pulitzer controlling interest of the *Westliche Post*. A few months later, the 25-year-old sold it back to Schurz and Preetorius for $30,000. He used part of that money to visit his mother in Hungary. He could assure her that he was safe and successful, as was his brother Albert, who had quit his teaching job in St. Louis to become a reporter for the *New York Sun*.

Pulitzer earned a decent living as a lawyer, but his heart remained in the publishing industry.

Narrow Escape

Joseph Pulitzer's thirtieth birthday party was very nearly his last. On April 10, 1877, he and his friends went out to celebrate the occasion before returning to his suite at the upscale Southern Hotel. Two hours later, the hotel was on fire.

Pulitzer managed to escape unharmed, but one of his companions died and another broke his leg jumping to safety. The fire killed several people and caused tremendous panic. The *New York Times* reported on the scene:

Owing to some neglect or delay, when the guests were aroused, almost every avenue of escape had been cut off by the suffocating smoke. Firemen and hotel employees ran through the halls kicking in doors and awakening the sleepers, but few of them were able to descend the stairways, and were driven back to their rooms, thus making escape from the windows the only means available. Then began a scene of the most agonizing and horrible nature. Men, women, and children appeared at the windows and eagerly bending down, wildly called for help.[4]

The fire department arrived too late to save the building, but with ropes and ladders, they rescued hundreds of residents.

Friends in High Places

Pulitzer did not have to pay a cent of his $400 fine for shooting attacker Edward Augustine in the leg at first. That was fortunate, because he had nowhere near that amount of money at the time. His political friends, including former mayor of St. Louis Daniel Taylor and Missouri Lieutenant Governor E. O. Stanard, paid the fine for him. Pulitzer eventually paid them all back.

He purchased the bankrupt *St. Louis Staats-Zeitung*, another German-language newspaper in St. Louis. He promptly sold it to the *St. Louis Globe* for a large profit. He was becoming financially ready to take a big step. And he was also ready to take a huge step in his personal life. Joseph Pulitzer was in love.

Carl Schurz, circa 1872

The St. Louis Post-Dispatch *building in 2005*

Marriage, Fame, and Fortune

By 1876, Joseph Pulitzer had gained great experience as both a writer and a politician. But he preferred to combine the two by writing about politics. And that year, he had the opportunity to do so for his favorite newspaper.

The *New York Sun* hired him as a special correspondent to cover the presidential election. Editor Charles A. Dana had turned down his request to start a German-language edition of the *Sun*, but he admired Pulitzer's talents as a journalist.

The new part-time job allowed Pulitzer to move temporarily to Washington DC. He covered the presidential race between Republican Rutherford B. Hayes and Democrat Samuel Tilden. Pulitzer enjoyed the experience not merely because he was covering a national election. It also gave him a chance to meet the woman of his dreams.

She Loved Him Back

In love with 23-year-old Kate Davis, Pulitzer moved permanently to Washington DC in 1877 and planned to practice law to be near her. Davis was an intelligent, wealthy, beautiful woman noted for her sense of humor. She was a distant cousin of Jefferson Davis, former president of the Confederacy.

Pulitzer was far from confident that a stunning woman with her background would marry him. He anxiously proposed, and Davis agreed to become his wife. Still, he was afraid she would change her mind. Pulitzer still had not settled on a career and thought

Kate would not want to be part of such uncertainty. After a brief quarrel, he took a business trip back to St. Louis. Frightened that she would end the engagement, he wrote her a love letter:

The Crooked Election

The 1876 presidential election that Pulitzer covered for the *New York Sun* was among the most controversial in U.S. history. The initial tally showed Democrat Samuel J. Tilden ahead by approximately 250,000 votes and leading in the electoral count, which is determined by the winners of individual states. Yet Republican Rutherford B. Hayes still became president.

Pulitzer revealed that Republicans threw out thousands of ballots in several states, particularly in Florida and Louisiana. In an attempt to satisfy angry Americans on both sides, Congress appointed a committee of seven Republicans, seven Democrats, and one independent——Supreme Court Justice David Davis—to decide the election.

Davis, however, retired and was replaced by Republican Joseph Bradley, which tilted the balance. The Republican majority switched the electoral votes, giving Hayes the presidency. That prompted angry Democrats, including Pulitzer, to call for a revolt. They held a protest meeting at Ford Theater, the site of President Lincoln's assassination in 1865. Pulitzer urged the crowd to arm themselves, but the revolt never materialized. The result was that Hayes served as president despite losing the election.

I am almost tired of this life—aimless, homeless, loveless; . . . I am impatient to turn over a new leaf and start a new life—one of which home must be the foundation, affection, ambition and occupation the corner stones, and you my dear, my inseparable companion. . . . I could not help thinking, I could not help feeling, how utterly selfish men are in love compared with women, when

I read your letter and feel its warmth. I cannot help saying that I am not worthy of such love, I am too cold and selfish, I know. Still, I am not without honor, and that alone would compel me to strive to become worthy of you, worthy of your faith and love, worthy of a better and finer future.[1]

His concerns that he was unworthy of her were unfounded. But he also feared that he would be rejected by her family had they known he was Jewish; her parents were upset enough that their daughter was marrying an immigrant with a thick accent. So, he kept his religion a secret until after their marriage at the Episcopal Church of the Epiphany in Washington DC on June 19, 1878.

A Publisher Emerges

On their return home, Pulitzer learned that the *St. Louis Dispatch* was nearly bankrupt, which allowed him to purchase it for the paltry sum of $2,500. His good fortune continued the next day when John Dillon, who owned the only rival evening newspaper, suggested that his *Evening Post* and Pulitzer's *Dispatch* merge

Foreign Correspondent

Pulitzer did not just spend time with new wife Kate on their honeymoon in Europe. He also agreed to write as a foreign correspondent for the *New York Sun*. Pulitzer visited England, France, and Germany. He wrote a series of articles about their governments and studied the lifestyles of their people.

rather than fight for readers. Pulitzer agreed under the condition that he had final say over the content of the newspaper. The deal was done, and the *St. Louis Post and Dispatch* was born.

Pulitzer laid out his approach to journalism in the first issue:

> *The* Post *and* Dispatch *will serve no party but the people; will be no organ of Republicanism, but the organ of the truth, will follow no caucuses but its own convictions; will not support the Administration, but criticize it; will oppose all frauds and shams wherever and whatever they are; will advocate principles and ideas rather than prejudices and partisanship.*[2]

At that point, Pulitzer began to show his brilliance as a publisher. Circulation skyrocketed when the paper printed the names of wealthy people who had falsified their tax returns. It continued to increase as the *Post-Dispatch*, which the paper had

Armed and Ready

Soon after purchasing the *Dispatch* and merging it with the *Post*, Pulitzer decided he needed protection from those who did not appreciate his crusading style of journalism. Convinced by his wife that others might attempt to do him bodily harm, Pulitzer bought a pistol and carried it with him throughout the day.

On one occasion in the late 1870s, Kate asked her husband to bring home a bag of tomatoes. As Pulitzer approached the house with the tomatoes, he recognized a thug who was approaching him with a menacing look. Rather than draw his gun at the assailant, he threw the tomatoes at him and rushed into the house. That was the last Pulitzer saw of the man.

Journalist Charles A. Dana, editor of the New York Sun

been renamed, began to specialize in stories about crime, violence, and the personal lives of well-known citizens.

Pulitzer was accused of sensationalism, but he responded that newspapers were morally obligated to expose crime and immorality. Such stories also sold newspapers and made him rich. Pulitzer soon grew even wealthier and more powerful when Dillon sold him his interest in the paper in November 1879 for $40,000. The circulation of the *Post-Dispatch* had more than doubled by the end of 1879. Pulitzer soon earned what was then an astronomical figure of at least $40,000 a year.

Pulitzer defended himself against charges of invasion of privacy and that he had gone too far in publishing the names of alleged tax evaders. Indeed, he argued that he had not gone far enough. "The tax returns are not private secrets; they are public documents," he wrote. "We would not willingly injure an honest man, but we do not care how many dishonest men are injured by the publication of their own sworn statements."[3]

PRESSURE ON THE JOB

The young publisher gained many enemies in exposing fraud and corruption, which made Kate worry about his safety. But the financial success of the *Post-Dispatch* allowed the couple to move to a home in an upscale neighborhood and start a family. Their son Ralph was born in June 1879, and Pulitzer began enjoying family life. He was no longer quite the workaholic he had been. Instead, he took off Sundays to spend with his family. Eventually, two daughters joined the family. Lucille was born in 1880, and Katherine was born in 1882.

As Pulitzer's family grew, so did his newspaper. The paper grew so much that Pulitzer added a managing editor, John Cockerill. But while Pulitzer was away from New York in 1882, tragedy struck the newspaper. Joseph, who was growing weaker due to the pressures of his work, took his family on a vacation to Europe in 1882. While he was gone, a man stormed into his office to violently protest an article written about him. Cockerill shot and killed the man.

The backlash proved catastrophic for Pulitzer. He rushed back to St. Louis. Public pressure forced him to fire Cockerill despite the findings that Cockerill had acted in self-defense. Many in St. Louis,

The *Post-Dispatch's* Fate

Though the *St. Louis Post-Dispatch* lost thousands of readers in the early 1880s, it did more than survive. It thrived. The *Post-Dispatch* is the only major paper in that city today and has been in existence for more than 130 years. While it has faced the same problems with declining circulation as other modern newspapers, in October 2008, it boasted a daily circulation of 241,796. Sunday circulation was more: 423,588.

including rival newspapers hungry to destroy the *Post-Dispatch*, claimed such a tragedy was an inevitable result of its sensationalism.

Pulitzer had not expected such an outcry. The circulation of his newspaper dropped dramatically. He struggled to find advertisers. He convinced Dillon, who had remained his friend, to take over as editor. Then he set out for Europe. He never reached the Atlantic Ocean. Fate was again about to send Joseph Pulitzer in a different direction. ⌐

An illustration shows Joseph Pulitzer with copies of the New York World *and the* St. Louis Post-Dispatch.

Albert Pulitzer, circa 1890

TAKING OVER THE *WORLD*

wning a major newspaper had become a
Pulitzer family affair by the early 1880s.
In November 1882, Joseph's brother Albert spent
$25,000 to launch the *New York Morning Journal*. While
Albert Pulitzer toiled to make his paper a success, his

brother Joseph struggled. The circulation of the *Post-Dispatch* was faltering, as was Joseph's health.

His doctor advised a long rest. Only after the newspaper started regaining circulation did Pulitzer agree to take time off. He decided to begin his vacation in New York City, where he planned to shop and see the sights. While in New York, he heard that the *New York World* was for sale and became obsessed with the thought of buying it. Its owner, Jay Gould, had earned a reputation for shady dealings and doing anything legally or illegally to make a profit. According to one biographer, "[Sly] and deadly as a spider, . . . Jay Gould fed on the betrayal of friends, fattened on the ruin of stockholders, lied and bribed his way to a power that raised him above the law."[1]

But the *World* was not one of Gould's successes. He was losing approximately $40,000 per year on the paper and was looking to dump it. However, he was not about to give it away. Gould was asking for more than half a million dollars; Pulitzer talked him down to $346,000. On May 9, 1883, the *World* was officially his.

New York Newspaper Prices

Albert Pulitzer sold his daily *New York Journal* to readers for just one cent per copy, the least expensive of all New York newspapers. Pulitzer's *World* cost two cents, as did the *Sun*, which in 1880 enjoyed the highest circulation in the city at 140,000. The *Herald* was three cents, while both the *Tribune* and the *Times* sold for four cents.

Pulitzer was determined to bring the same crusading style to the *World* that had made the *Post-Dispatch* a huge success. Pulitzer's editorial in his first issue informed readers of his plans. He wrote,

There is room in this great and growing city for a journal that is not only cheap but bright, not only bright but large, not only large but truly democratic— dedicated to the cause of the people rather than the [rich]—devoted more to the news of the New than the Old World—that will expose all fraud and sham, fight all public evils and abuses—

The New Journalism

The groundbreaking ideas Pulitzer implemented at the *World* made him one of the most important players in the creation of what was called the new journalism. Pulitzer ran sensational stories and headlines alongside serious, in-depth news coverage. He used strong editorial pages and attention-grabbing stunts to crusade for his ideals. Other innovations included the use of drawings to illustrate stories and the introduction of sports coverage to make his paper appeal more to the average reader.

Newspaper owners around the country took their leads from Pulitzer and tried to duplicate his success at their own papers. U.S. journalist and historian Frank Luther Mott wrote about Pulitzer's great influence on his profession in the book *American Journalism*:

No wonder newspaper publishers everywhere studied the World *and imitated its policies until a New Journalism grew out of them. An acute observer wrote in 1887 that the* World *had "affected the character of the entire daily press of the country." The "wild Missourian," as the Kansas City* Journal *called Pulitzer, had upset the status quo and furnished a new formula for the metropolitan daily.[2]*

that will serve and battle for the people with earnest sincerity.[3]

Pulitzer broke new ground by appealing to the huge influx of immigrants in New York, many of whom could barely read English. He used pictures and huge headlines to draw attention to colorfully written stories. He instructed his reporters to use strong but simple language, eye-catching headlines, and short sentences so the stories and articles could be understood by the masses.

Immigrant Audience

From a financial standpoint, Pulitzer was wise to gear his newspaper to the immigrant population of New York at that time. During the early 1880s, approximately 500,000 immigrants entered the United States annually. Most were transported into New York Harbor, and many of them remained in New York City.

Beginning of a Revolution

Pulitzer lured former *Post-Dispatch* managing editor John Cockerill from St. Louis to New York. Despite the shooting incident, he believed Cockerill to be a great editor. Pulitzer then set out to revolutionize the newspaper industry. The *World* splashed stories about violence, scandal, tragedy, and crime throughout its pages, but Pulitzer insisted on careful accuracy. He combined these splashy stories with serious coverage of important issues.

He also brought a crusading style from St. Louis to New York. While he did want to make sure the newspaper was profitable, he cared more about using journalism as a force for social change. Pulitzer encouraged his reporters to maintain a crusade about something at all times, whether it was eliminating political corruption, exposing criminal activity, raising money for charitable causes, or improving the school system. Pulitzer paid special attention to the editorial pages, where he promoted his many crusades.

Pulitzer also unveiled special sections that attracted new readers. Understanding the interests of workingmen, he began a daily sports section. He started features on fashion and social life for women. He was the first to consistently run a comics page.

One of his editors, James Townsend, later described the effect that Pulitzer had on the newsroom at the *World* and on New York journalism as a whole:

Sensational Stories

No story that was supposedly confirmed was too wild to be published in Pulitzer's *World*. In early Sunday editions of the paper, Pulitzer ran stories on cannibalism at sea, human sacrifice in the United States by fanatical religious groups, and odd murder weapons such as a red-hot horseshoe, an umbrella, and a teakettle. Some stories stretched the imagination but could not be disproved given the technology of the nineteenth century. The *World* even ran a report about a French scientist supposedly uncovering a tribe of people with well-developed tails.

Joseph Pulitzer, 1880s

In a week's time the new **World** *under Joseph Pulitzer was a bull in the china shop of New York journalism. It began to smash traditions, customs, and ideas like the proverbial* *animal did the china. The public first gasped, then condemned or admired the new journalism.*[4]

Presidential Endorsement

Many believe that Pulitzer was responsible for putting Democrat Grover Cleveland in the White House in 1884. Pulitzer ran the only Democratic newspaper in New York City. The *World* vigorously endorsed Cleveland during the campaign. He won New York by just 1,149 votes, which gave him all 36 of the state's electoral votes. If 575 popular votes for Cleveland had gone the other way, Republican James Blaine would have become president. That same election day, Pulitzer received 15,518 votes, almost double the number earned by Republican Herman Thum, to earn a Congressional seat. Pulitzer resigned from Congress after four months.

The circulation of the Sunday edition of the *World* before Pulitzer bought it was approximately 15,000. Two years later, circulation had swelled to more than 150,000. The *World* was now among the most-read newspapers in the United States. That alone did not satisfy Pulitzer. While working endlessly at the *World*, he made time to run for Congress in 1884. His victory required that he travel back and forth between New York and Washington DC.

This left him little time for a family that was growing as quickly as his newspaper. Daughter Katherine died of pneumonia just six weeks before her second birthday in 1884. Kate gave birth to their son Joseph Jr. in 1885, daughter Edith in 1886, and daughter Constance in 1888.

Jay Gould, who sold the New York World *to Pulitzer*

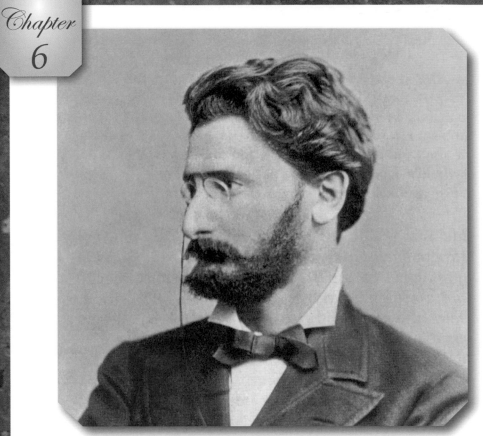

Joseph Pulitzer at age 40

New Ideas Pay Off

As his family grew and his career reached its height, Pulitzer continued to suffer from health problems. He could not sleep and suffered from asthma. He was exhausted. He quickly flew into a rage at the slightest provocation.

Doctors urged him to rest, but he was determined to move ahead with his journalism work. However, he did resign his post in Congress after four months.

Pulitzer visited health spas in Europe, but he could not stop thinking and worrying about his business. Rather than simply allow his staff to run the newspaper, he would have the *World* mailed to him, and he critiqued every section. He would then send a barrage of critical letters and cables to his editors with his orders spelled out.

PATRIOTIC PROJECT

Pulitzer's crusades also continued. The United States was celebrating Independence Day in 1884 when a gift from France was presented in Paris to Levi Moron, the U.S. Minister to France. It was a magnificent 151-foot (46-m) monument that became known the

Charitable Side

Though Pulitzer was considered by many to be greedy, with a chief motivation to make money, he also proved to be quite charitable. He gave generously to several causes as well as to friends who needed help. In early 1886 alone, he donated to the New York Sanitary Aid Society, gave to a Catholic charity, and contributed to the Roosevelt Hospital. He paid for the college education of the sons of William Patrick, who had helped Pulitzer in his law career. Pulitzer also sent money to a struggling librarian friend, Udo Brachvogel.

world over as Lady Liberty. The statue symbolized the freedoms enjoyed by all Americans.

However, there was one problem. A home, Bedloe's Island in New York Harbor, had been designated for the statue. However, the statue needed a platform on which to stand. Though a committee had raised $100,000 for a pedestal on which to place the Statue of Liberty, it was not nearly enough to cover the costs. The 16.5-foot (5-m) torch-bearing hand had been shown in Philadelphia eight years earlier. The 17-foot (5.2-m) head remained in Paris. And now the structure had been dismantled and placed in 214 crates during transport to New York.

Pulitzer sprang into action. He revered the liberty and freedom for which the United States stood. He also yearned to increase circulation. So his newspaper began yet another crusade by launching a campaign

Help from the
Post-Dispatch

The *World* was not the only newspaper to spearhead the effort to raise money to build a platform for the Statue of Liberty. The *St. Louis Post-Dispatch* did the same. Though Pulitzer concentrated his efforts on the *World* after purchasing it in 1883, he still owned the *Post-Dispatch*, which also donated to the campaign.

to raise money for a pedestal for the statue. On March 16, 1885, an editorial asking all New Yorkers to contribute was splashed across the paper:

> *It would be an irrevocable disgrace to New York City and the American Republic to have France send us this splendid gift without our having provided even so much as a landing place for it. . . . There is but one thing that can be done. We must raise the money. The* World *is the people's paper, and it now appeals to the people to come forward and raise this money. The $250,000 that the . . . statue cost was paid in by the masses of the French people—by the workingmen, the tradesmen, the shop girls, the artisans— by all, irrespective of class or condition. Let us respond in like manner. Let us not wait for the millionaires to give this money. It is not a gift from the millionaires of France to the millionaires of America but a gift*

Pulitzer's Temper

Pulitzer's temper got the best of him in 1887 after he pulled *World* reporter Joseph Howard off a coveted assignment—a winter carnival in Montreal. Howard tried to talk Pulitzer into allowing him to cover the Canadian event, but to no avail. An argument ensued, after which both started throwing punches. By some accounts, Pulitzer grabbed Howard's collar and pants and literally tossed him out of the office. That was Howard's last day working at the *New York World*.

of the whole people of France to the whole people of America.

Take this appeal to yourself personally. . . . Give something, however little. . . . let us hear from the people.[1]

Pulitzer's goal was soon accomplished. He began the drive himself by contributing $250. Donations ranging from five cents to $1,000 poured in from all over the nation from 120,000 different donors. In less than five months, people throughout the country had raised the extra $100,000 needed to build a pedestal for the Statue of Liberty.

Bringing in Bly

In terms of sensationalism and creativity, few Pulitzer schemes topped his use of a 23-year-old woman named Elizabeth Cochrane as an undercover reporter in 1887. Desperate for work, Cochrane talked her way into Cockerill's office looking for a job.

Pulitzer learned about the young woman and decided she was ideal for a project he had been considering for months. He wanted to investigate an insane asylum on nearby Blackwell Island that had been allegedly mistreating its patients. Cochrane

Nellie Bly, circa 1890

had been using the alias Nellie Bly. She suggested that using that name, she feign insanity and check herself in as a patient. Pulitzer believed an exposé could shame asylum officials into treating its patients more humanely. One problem remained. Once Bly had been certified as a lunatic, how was she to get out of the institution? Pulitzer promised to rescue her after her job was completed.

Bly rehearsed for her coming performance, as would an actress. She checked herself into a boarding house for women and began acting crazy. The day after she arrived, one of the frightened residents called a police officer, who brought Bly before a judge. She was then examined by experts at Bellevue Hospital and sent to the

More about Nellie

The performance of Nellie Bly in the insane asylum exposé so impressed Pulitzer that he eventually hired her full-time. Bly was among the few female reporters involved in investigative journalism at major papers in the United States in the late 1800s.

Bly enhanced her credentials in 1888 when she used various modes of transportation to travel around the globe in a world-record 72 days. The publicity stunt was inspired by the Jules Verne book *Around the World in Eighty Days*. During her trip, she visited England, France, Egypt, Japan, Hong Kong, and China. In 1895, the 30-year-old Bly married millionaire Robert Seaman, who was 40 years older. She quit journalism to become president of the Iron Clad Manufacturing Company. Her husband died in 1904, but by that time Bly had become one of the foremost female industrialists in the country.

Her business eventually faltered, however, and Bly faced bankruptcy. She returned to journalism and reported on events such as World War I in Europe and the suffrage movement that worked for women's right to vote. Bly died of pneumonia in 1922 at the age of 57.

insane asylum on Blackwell Island. Bly went to work immediately. She spent ten days in the asylum and wrote about the barely edible food, terrible conditions, and abusive nurses.

The reaction after the exposé had been published in the *World* was swift and decisive. A grand jury launched an investigation of the asylum with Bly's assistance. It pushed through all the changes Bly had recommended, as well as additional funding for the care of the insane.

SKYROCKETING NUMBERS

By the end of 1887, Pulitzer claimed the *World* was the most read newspaper on Earth. It boasted an average daily circulation of 317,940—more than three times greater than that of its archrival, the *Sun*. But while Pulitzer's professional life thrived, his health continued to deteriorate. One day while Pulitzer was reading editorial copy that was to be printed the next day, he noticed that he was struggling to make out the words. He assumed it was due to some temporary cause, but he soon found out he was going blind. To slow the onset, the doctor demanded that he spend the next six weeks in a darkened room. Though a workaholic, Pulitzer

understood that blindness could end his career, so
he heeded the doctor's advice.

Following those six weeks, another examination
revealed that Pulitzer had a ruptured blood vessel
in one eye. He was told to relax for six months in
the California sun. The thought of six months away
from work was torturous for Pulitzer, but again
he complied. When that failed to cure his various
ailments, he took off for Europe to consult with
specialists. Each reiterated what U.S. doctors had
been suggesting: that he retire from the newspaper
industry and take it easy. But this went against
Pulitzer's ambitious nature.

Going against his doctors' advice, Pulitzer
returned to work at the *New York World*. He directed
the newspaper's coverage of the 1888 state and
national elections. He did attempt to make his
personal life less stressful by purchasing a country
home in Bar Harbor, Maine. A soundproof tower
was built to eliminate the noise he could no longer
bear, including the cries of new daughter Constance.
As his eyesight began failing, his hearing became
painfully oversensitive.

Cartoonist Thomas Nast created this pencil sketch of Joseph Pulitzer during Pulitzer's time at the New York World.

The domed Pulitzer Building, left, is pictured between 1900 and 1910.

ACTS OF DESPERATION

Joseph Pulitzer was only 42 years old. But he was forced to take precautions with his frail health. Warned by one doctor not to bend over because it could result in a brain artery rupture, he never again tied his own shoes.

In 1889, he set sail with two doctors and two acquaintances through the Middle East and Asia. And though secretary Claude Ponsonby wrote optimistically to Pulitzer's wife Kate about her husband's potential recovery, Pulitzer challenged that notion in his own letters to his wife. While in India, he expressed his misery to Kate:

> *I really feel that my health is broken . . . and that I cannot in reason expect to regain it without either that freedom from all business worry and care and the enjoyment of that domestic care and peace which seem beyond my reach. Travel will not cure me. I am miserable. I cannot trust myself to write more. Whatever I feel however, you are still the only being in this world who fills my heart and mind and hope and receives my love and tenderness and affection.[1]*

Pulitzer hoped he could continue his work at the *World*. He consulted

One Doctor's Assessment

One doctor who saw Pulitzer's physical deterioration firsthand was George Hosmer. He spent a great deal of energy attempting to shield Pulitzer from any news regarding the *World*. Hosmer wrote of Pulitzer, "He was very ill—in a state so feeble that he could scarcely get around on foot. He passed days on a sofa . . . it was a physical strain for him to cross the room and sit at the table. . . . Physical collapse had assumed the form of nervous [exhaustion] . . . directly due to his intense efforts in building up the *World*."[2]

**Investigation
of Elmira Prison**

In 1892, Pulitzer contin-
ued to use his clout to
attempt to bring justice
to the world around him.
Pulitzer launched a cam-
paign to end reported
abuse at nearby Elmira
Prison. He had received
reports that warden Zebu-
lon Brockway was still
flogging prisoners. When
Pulitzer became con-
vinced that it was true, the
World started a campaign
to have Brockway fired.
However, the campaign
was not successful.

Philadelphia neurologist Silas
Weir Mitchell hoping to find relief
for his ailments so that he could
throw himself back into his work.
But Mitchell ordered the stunned
Pulitzer to cease all contact with the
newspaper. Mitchell further advised
that he rest after meals, exercise daily,
have a massage before bedtime to help
him sleep, and embark on another
long boat trip to avoid stress.

On October 16, 1890, the
newspaper announced that Pulitzer
had withdrawn from his editorship.
Though he would remain as owner of
the newspaper, he would no longer
supervise its content. The control
of the *World* was placed in the hands
of an executive board made up of
trusted veterans of the newspaper.
Shocked rivals and journalists across
the country expressed their dismay in
unison. They praised Pulitzer for his
influence on the newspaper industry
and for his perseverance.

AVOIDING RETIREMENT

But those who truly believed Pulitzer could cut off all contact with the *World* were mistaken. Pulitzer was nearly blind and plagued with asthma, insomnia, diabetes, migraine headaches, and depression. Still, he would remain in charge of his newspaper. The stormiest and greatest years of his career still lay ahead.

On December 10, 1890, the grand opening of the spectacular new domed *World* building took place. The 20-floor building was 309 feet (94 m) high, making it the tallest structure in the country at the time. It even featured bedroom apartments on the eleventh floor for editors and reporters who worked into the wee hours of the morning.

Pulitzer began complaining to Doctor Mitchell that his inactivity was driving him crazy. Then Pulitzer was told that the executives at the *World* were fighting for control, ignoring their work in the process, and causing the newspaper to fall apart. Pulitzer ignored his doctor's demands.

Special Edition

Pulitzer was not in New York when the *World* honored him with a 100-page edition on May 7, 1893. He was returning from Europe, and the ship would not arrive until three days later. The issue was to commemorate Pulitzer's ten-year anniversary as owner of the newspaper. It sold a record 400,000 copies.

He sailed back to New York after a short rest in Europe to shake things up at the *World* once more. He then initiated a system that would allow him to remain in complete control of the newspaper no matter where he was. He sent cables to stay in constant communication with his staff and even developed an elaborate code so that the contents of the messages remained secret.

Mitchell warned Pulitzer that if he continued to work it would "inevitably result in destruction of what remains of your eyesight." He added,

> It is quite impossible for you to carry on your paper under present conditions without total sacrifice of your general health. The course on which you are now engaged is one of physical disaster.[3]

Pulitzer once again ignored the warning. He directed the coverage of the 1892 election, supervised new managing editor George Harvey, created a team to run the paper that he called the "World Council," and ordered financial director Solomon Carvalho to cut costs.

In his ongoing search for the ideal combination of tranquility and professional satisfaction, Pulitzer left for France in late 1893. He found a home in the town of Nice, France, which would be free of barking dogs, traffic, and chattering neighbors.

Soon he was housed in a huge mansion overlooking the Mediterranean Sea. Pulitzer had it soundproofed and hired aides to read to him, tend to his comfort, and keep him informed of the news as well as of the daily contents of his newspaper. They were instructed to send his comments and orders to his staff at the *World*. These aides enabled him to continue running the *World* despite his difficulties.

In early summer 1894, Pulitzer returned to his country home in Maine and hired Felix Webber as a secretary and a piano player. Webber was

Parting Ways

Few, if any, working companions were closer to Pulitzer than *World* editor in chief John Cockerill. Nearly all who worked for Pulitzer were obligated to refer to him as Mr. Pulitzer, but Cockerill simply called him Joe.

In 1891, however, the professional relationship between the two men fell apart. Cockerill sought a greater stake in the newspaper's rapidly growing profits and more praise for his work. Pulitzer refused to give him either.

Their relationship worsened. The two began to fight frequently, which prompted Pulitzer to ask Cockerill to return to St. Louis and take over the editorship at the *Post-Dispatch*. Cockerill refused and resigned. Soon he landed a job as editor of the *Morning Advertiser*.

In later years, Pulitzer yearned to bring Cockerill back, but to no avail. When Cockerill died in 1896, Pulitzer spoke of his old friend with tremendous respect. He described him as "handsome and intellectual, a fighter if there was fighting to be done, [and] infinitely proud of being a newspaperman."[4]

disgusted by Pulitzer's behavior, particularly his relationship with his family. The new aide recalled one incident after 14-year-old daughter Lucille had undergone throat surgery. Kate remained by her bedside, but Pulitzer never spent a moment with the sick girl. Webber added that the shaken Kate asked her husband why he had not visited Lucille and why he did not seem to pity her.

According to Webber, Pulitzer shouted back at his wife,

> *Pity Lucille! No! I'm the only one to pity—has no one any pity for me!—does no one realize what I suffer! My own house turned into a hospital! Doctors coming at all hours! You rushing upstairs in the middle of meals, without a word of conversation for me. No one pities me and you ask me to pity Lucille!*[5]

Pulitzer felt guilty about his outburst the next day and spent time with his daughter. He also instructed Webber to spare no expense in traveling to New York and buying Lucille a basket of roses.

Pulitzer led an investigation of Elmira Prison in 1892.

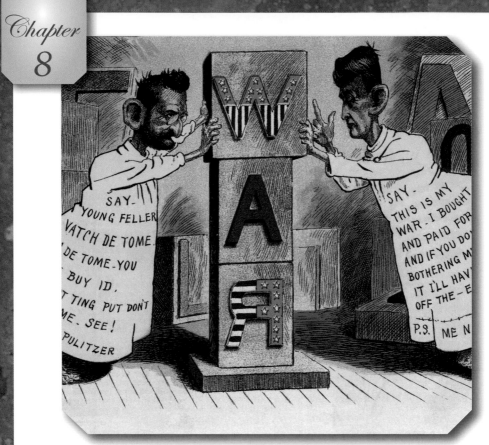

A cartoon drawn in 1898 shows the conflict between Joseph Pulitzer and William Randolph Hearst.

SHAME, SPAIN, AND THE *MAINE*

As the nineteenth century neared its end, few would have contested that Joseph Pulitzer was the most influential publisher in the United States. But most would not have believed that he wielded enough power to prevent war.

That changed in December 1895, the month after
Pulitzer's youngest son, Herbert, was born.

The conflict brewing between the United States
and Great Britain centered on a 50-year-old border
dispute between Venezuela and the British colony
of Guyana. When gold was discovered in the area,
both South American countries claimed it. The
Venezuelan government asked the United States
to help.

President Grover Cleveland warned the British
not to get involved. He cited the Monroe Doctrine,
which was written in 1823. It specified that no
European nation could interfere with U.S. interests
anywhere in the Western Hemisphere. But British
Prime Minister Lord Salisbury pointed out that
Guyana had belonged to England before Venezuela
even existed.

Cleveland reacted angrily. He asserted that
Britain was threatening U.S. peace and safety.
Congress authorized a commission to investigate
the border dispute between British Guyana and
Venezuela. The two countries seemed headed toward
a military conflict. Many Americans believed war
was justified, and their newspapers generally echoed
those sentiments.

BUCKING THE TREND

The *World* took a different stance. Pulitzer launched a campaign for peace. The newspaper ran editorials stating that going to war against a nation that had been a friend, over a border dispute thousands of miles away, was madness. Pulitzer sent hundreds of cables to British political and religious leaders, including one to Lord Salisbury and another to former Prime Minister William Gladstone that read:

> *American sentiment is at the turning point. Once turned the wrong way, no power on earth will hold it back. . . . A word of peace and fellowship from you today will aid to check the clamor, to soothe passion, to encourage sober thought, and may avert calamity.*[1]

Gladstone simply replied that Pulitzer should not interfere, but the *World* responded by publishing dozens of letters from British officials urging

Modern Man

Pulitzer was ahead of his time in many ways. Among them was the use of motorized delivery trucks to deliver the *World* around New York. The *World* was the first New York City newspaper to utilize them. He purchased the first motorized vehicle for $2,000 and eventually bought 20 more before his competitors had any. The purchase put 70 delivery horses out of work.

peace. U.S. leaders still called for war, but Pulitzer had softened their message. Venezuela ended any threat of war by handing nearly all of the disputed area over to the British. Britain Colonial Secretary Joseph Chamberlain expressed his thanks to Pulitzer:

> *War between the two countries would be a terrible calamity, and the* World *performed a patriotic service to its country. It did not wait for a leader, but led the people.*[2]

Pulitzer appeared far less honorable and peace loving when a conflict arose with another European country. This time his motivation was not saving the world from war, but selling more newspapers.

The seeds were planted when multimillionaire William Randolph Hearst purchased the rival *New York Journal*, which was once owned by Pulitzer's brother, Albert. Hearst played a game of copycat, transforming his newspaper into a mirror image of the *World*. Hearst had studied the *World* as he ran his first paper, the *San Francisco Examiner*. He understood why Pulitzer's paper had blossomed into the most popular in the United States. So he set out to duplicate it through sensationalism, crusades, and support of the underdog in U.S. society.

Portrait of William Randolph Hearst, circa 1906

The *Journal* hit the newsstands at just one cent per copy, half the price of the *World*. Soon the daily *Journal* circulation had skyrocketed to 150,000 while the *World's* circulation ceased to grow. Meanwhile, Hearst raided Pulitzer's staff by offering them more money and lured many of them away. Pulitzer reacted by reducing the cost of his paper to one cent.

The competition between the papers became fierce. In the battle to win readers, Pulitzer tossed away his journalistic principles, including his demand for accuracy. He ordered his staff to find wild stories even if they required exaggeration or complete fabrication. In the next several months, both papers were accused of stealing each other's stories. The era of yellow journalism, another name for sensationalized or even untruthful reporting, had begun.

CIRCULATION WAR

The circulation war between the *Journal* and the *World* began in earnest in 1896. It revolved around the Cuban rebellion against Spain. Hearst published reports about atrocities committed by the Spanish in its attempt to quell the uprising. Many of the accounts were distorted or completely false, but they sold papers. Pulitzer's writers had at first

Yellow Journalism

During his circulation war with the *World*, Hearst lured away *World* cartoonist Richard Felton Outcault, the creator of a wildly popular comic strip called "Hogan's Alley." The cartoon featured a mischievous child nicknamed the Yellow Kid. Pulitzer was forced to discontinue the strip, which reappeared on the front page of the *Journal*. Pulitzer responded by creating a strip featuring the Yellow Kid's twin brother. Meanwhile, *New York Press* editor Ervin Wardman searched for a term to describe the sensationalism of the *World* and the *Journal*. He considered the strip and then came up with "yellow journalism." The term stuck.

been factual in their reporting of the crisis. Now, he ordered them to produce bloodier accounts to keep up with the *Journal*.

The result was catastrophic. Neither Spain nor the United States sought war. But when the U.S. battleship *Maine* blew up off the Cuban shores, both newspapers blamed the Spanish without investigating the facts. Spain claimed that the explosion that killed 266 Americans was caused internally, but the stories in the *World* and the *Journal* motivated the United States to declare war on Spain.

Above the Fray

Most New York newspapers refused to follow the lead of the *World* and the *Journal* during the Spanish-American War. The *New York Times*, with a circulation of just 10,000, could not afford to send correspondents to the action and was forced to use Associated Press dispatches. The *Times* ran an editorial claiming that the Spanish government would never have destroyed the *Maine*.

The drive to sell newspapers at the cost of journalistic integrity paid off financially. The day after President William McKinley declared war on Spain in 1898, both papers sold an estimated 1.3 million copies.

The Spanish–American War lasted less than four months. The majority of the 5,000 Americans who died lost their lives to diseases such as malaria and typhoid. The war resulted with the U.S. occupation of Cuba, Puerto Rico, Guam, and the Philippines.

But Pulitzer had lost something far more important—his credibility. Pulitzer learned his lesson. He not only regretted forgetting his principles during his circulation war with Hearst for moral reasons, but he also realized it did not earn him any more money. Though he sold far more papers, the costs in covering the war wiped out his profits. Eighteen reporters had been hired, and three press boats had been dispatched to take his correspondents from one battle to the next.

In November 1898, Pulitzer summoned his top editors and insisted that the

Leaving Yellow Journalism Behind

Pulitzer did not merely claim that he had learned a lesson from the yellow journalism period and circulation war with the *New York Journal*. He proved it early in 1899. One opportunity to show that he and the *World* had regained their journalistic ethics occurred after a woman named Martha Place gained national attention. She murdered her stepdaughter and then attempted to kill her husband with an ax. Place soon became the first woman executed by electric chair.

Both the *World* and the *Journal* gave the story plenty of attention. But Hearst's paper splashed a sketch of Place dying in the electric chair and claimed in the accompanying story that she died in tortured agony. Pulitzer, on the other hand, insisted that the *World* cover the event accurately. The *World* wrote that Place died appearing brave and seemed to die instantly and without pain. As proof of that assertion, the *World* quoted a witness who claimed Place's pulse was regular and that she displayed no evidence of suffering. And rather than show a sketch of Place on the electric chair, the *World* ran a copy of her prayer book.

World return to its prewar policy of truth, fairness, and accuracy in its reporting. They, in turn, passed the word on to the rest of the staff. Editor William Van Benthuysen told his underlings in no uncertain terms:

> *Every bit of copy you write, every line you edit and send to the copy desk, every picture you draw, every bit of news given, make it absolutely accurate so that it is not to be denied the next day. We must all work unceasingly together to produce the greatest newspaper in the land. Sensational? Yes, when the news is sensational. But it must never be forgotten that every story which is sensational in itself must also be truthful.* [3]

A few years later, Pulitzer would lend his name to an annual award presented to journalists whose performance best exemplified those same ideals.

Joseph Pulitzer

EXPLOSION CAUSED BY BOMB OR TO

e and Consul-General Lee Are in Doubt---The World

g, With Submarine Divers, to Havana to Find Out---Lee

Immediate Court of Inquiry---Capt. Sigsbee's Suspicion

UPPRESSED DESPATCH TO THE STATE DEPARTMENT, SAYS THE ACCIDENT WAS MADE POSS

Just Arrived from Havana, Says He Overheard Talk There of a Plot to Blow U

the Dynamite Expert, and Other Experts Report to The World that the Wreck

cidental---Washington Officials Ready for Vigorous Action if Spanish Responsibili

Can Be Shown---Divers to Be Sent Down to Make Careful Examinations.

The front page of the New York World *shows the newspaper's coverage of the Maine explosion.*

An issue of the New York World *published June 25, 1906*

BACK TO TRUTH
AND ACCURACY

The world had just entered the twentieth century when a new tragedy struck the Pulitzer home. On January 9, workmen noticed smoke pouring out of Pulitzer's Manhattan house. Joseph was in New Jersey with Joe, and Ralph was at school, but the rest of the family was still in bed. Kate awoke and began to choke from the smoke. She rushed to the third-floor bedrooms of 13-year-old Constance, 11-year-old Edith, and 4-year-old Herbert.

Kate screamed for everyone to follow her, and the group managed to escape. They stood outside in the freezing temperature until a neighbor took them in. Housekeeper Morgan Jellett and governess Elizabeth Montgomery both perished in the blaze that destroyed the house. The Pulitzers temporarily stayed at the Netherlands Hotel until they moved into a much larger house in Manhattan.

In September 1901, the country was struck with a far greater tragedy. President McKinley was shot and killed at the Pan-American Exposition in Buffalo, New York. Staff members had warned him to cancel his appearance due to a *World* story reporting rumors of an assassination plot. But McKinley had shrugged off the warnings.

Some believed Hearst was responsible for McKinley's death. They cited an editorial in the *Journal* that read, "If bad institutions and bad men can be got rid of only by killing, then the killing must be done."[1] And after the murder of Kentucky

Governor William Goebel, the *Journal* ran a poem by Ambrose Bierce indicating the bullet that murdered Goebel was on its way to kill McKinley as well.

The newspapers' coverage before and after the president's murder spotlighted the new differences between the philosophies of Pulitzer and Hearst.

Pulitzer sent his personal doctor to Buffalo to report on the condition of McKinley, who suffered two bullet wounds. Following the president's death, Pulitzer reminded his staff to stick to factual reporting.

In this case, Hearst's sensationalism did not achieve the desired results. Blamed by many for

Joseph Pulitzer Jr.

In 1891, Pulitzer's 16-year-old son Joe was expelled from his prep school in Massachusetts. Joe had left the grounds after curfew to buy beer but then could not get back into the building. So he climbed into an open window, only to find that he had shocked the headmaster and his wife in their bedroom!

Upon learning his son had been kicked out of school, Pulitzer was furious. He sent an angry note to Kate:

It is not the incident, but the causes. The character, the loss of moral sense and loss of honor involved in it. . . . He has very little mind, very little intelligence, very little head but a great deal of animal instinct, a great deal of passion for pleasure and nothing else. No respectable aims, no high ambitions, aspirations, ideas, tastes so far as I can see, except for physical pleasures.[2]

From that moment forward, Pulitzer monitored his son's every move. The strategy worked—Joe eventually embarked on a brilliant career in journalism.

McKinley's assassination, the *Journal* lost thousands of subscribers. Advertisers left in droves. New Yorkers snatched copies of the paper from newsboys and burned them. Demonstrators in cities around the country torched stuffed likenesses of Hearst.

STABBED IN THE BACK

Pulitzer certainly was not immune to criticism. In 1901, *World* editor and columnist David Graham Phillips published a book titled *The Great God Success*. The main character, Howard, was based on Pulitzer. Early in the book, Howard is idealistic and enthusiastic about journalism. But as the story progresses, he becomes hateful and greedy. His genuine desire to help the common man is overtaken by his desire to make money. And he ends up rich but miserable.

The portrayal of Pulitzer was accurate in that he was indeed wealthy and unhappy. But most who were close to him believed that, aside

Standing Against Racism

One incident in 1901 caused Pulitzer to show his moral outrage. President Theodore Roosevelt had invited famed black educator Booker T. Washington to a luncheon in the White House. Several journalists in the South, where racial prejudice was still rampant, reacted with anger. Pulitzer reacted with anger in turn. "An American named Washington, one of the most learned, most eloquent, most brilliant men of his day . . . is asked to dinner by President Roosevelt," he wrote, "and because the pigment of his skin is some shades darker than that of others a large part of the United States is convulsed with shame and rage. . . . Should [Liberty] weep?"[3]

A 1955 photo of Joseph Pulitzer II, son of Joseph Pulitzer and editor and publisher of the St. Louis Post-Dispatch *for 43 years*

from the yellow journalism period of the late 1890s, he had maintained his ideals. They also felt that Pulitzer was again vigorously stressing accuracy and truthfulness in the *World*.

The gap between honest and dishonest journalism widened in the autumn of 1902 when Hearst financed a massive fireworks display near the famed Madison Square Garden. A firework exploded

prematurely and set off several
more. Nineteen people were killed,
including a police officer. More than
50 others were injured. Every paper
in town ran a story about the tragedy
on the front page. But Hearst, who
was trying to win a seat in Congress,
had it buried on page five with no
word of his connection to the event.

Pulitzer continued on a righteous
journalistic path. He made an offer
to Nicholas Murray Butler, president
of Columbia University in New York,
to fund the nation's first journalism school. Pulitzer
provided an endowment of $2 million to make it
happen. Eventually, the dream of college students
preparing for a journalism career from the most
learned journalism professors in the country became
a reality. And so did an annual award to the nation's
journalists that would bear Pulitzer's name.

Looking to the Future

Pulitzer created a rather special feature for the first issue of the *World* in the twentieth century. It was an artist's rendition of what New York City might look like in 1999. The drawing turned out to be incredibly accurate. It was almost identical to how the city appeared as the new millennium approached, including the many skyscrapers. All that was missing was Central Park.

CELEBRATION OF SUCCESS

Pulitzer was proud of what he had accomplished
in the 20 years he had owned the *World*, and he
wanted to make the anniversary of his purchase

special. On May 10, 1903, a 136-page edition of the newspaper celebrated its many triumphs and restated its moral and political priorities. This included Pulitzer's insistence on accuracy and the championing of freedom and democracy for all. It also proudly proclaimed that it had earned an income of $67 million and a profit of $21 million during that time, while increasing its circulation from 9,669 to 518,707.

The edition also featured a quote from Pulitzer. He wrote:

> *The highest satisfaction felt by the director of the* World *in its success comes from the reflection that it has not been won by any sacrifice of principle, any surrender of conviction, any appeal to party spirit or class prejudice.*[4]

Equally impressive was a quote from former president Cleveland, who stated that although

> *[I have] quite often differed with the* World *very broadly, I would, however, be ashamed if any difference between us made it difficult for me to cheerfully testify to the notable service which this great newspaper has rendered within the last twenty years, to the cause of democracy.*[5]

An illustration shows Joseph Pulitzer holding a press
printing the New York World in 1901.

The final copies of the morning and evening editions of the New York World *are presented to the Los Angeles Public Library in 1931.*

DEATH OF A PUBLISHING GIANT

t 57, Joseph Pulitzer had the physical ailments most often associated with people 30 years his senior. He was blind in his right eye and suffered from pounding headaches. He could barely sleep. He required his valet to dress him.

Despite these ailments, Pulitzer's large staff enabled him to stay active and involved. His companions at home or abroad included four secretaries, his personal physician, and one assistant. He was required to take a nap every afternoon but could only nod off while being read to in a soft voice. More reading and the soothing strains of classical music gave him his only chance to fall asleep at night.

Such was Pulitzer's lot in life a few years into the twentieth century. By that time, he was contemplating his legacy. How would he be remembered once he was gone? Among those who believed Pulitzer would have made an even greater mark in the political world had he remained healthy was Adolph Ochs, publisher of the *New York Times.* Ochs had transformed his paper into one of the most popular in the world. He later wrote in praise of Pulitzer:

Times Tribute

Following the death of Pulitzer, the *New York Times* published a lengthy front-page story. In addition to chronicling his life, it detailed his continued influence despite his failing health and need to travel: "He had been obliged to spend much of his time abroad or at his country seat at Bar Harbor. But his hand was felt directing the destinies of the *World,* no matter in what corner of the globe he happened to be. . . . No man kept more closely in touch with what was going on in the world, and all the information had to come to him by word of mouth. He could not read; he could not distinguish the faces of those about him. He could only listen and think."[1]

[Pulitzer is] a man of great strength and great intellectual power, and of education and culture. He is a man among thousands. He is positive, well informed on current topics, truly a philosopher. It is a great and tragic misfortune that he is virtually blind. If he had not that affliction he would be a tremendous figure in national affairs. [2]

That Pulitzer was mindful of his legacy became apparent when his rival Hearst ran for governor of New York in 1906. Hearst made hateful speeches about his critics, who lashed back with the accusation that he was responsible for the assassination

End of the *World*

The death of Joseph Pulitzer did not mean the death of the *New York World*. But the newspaper never again reached its previous heights. Pulitzer handed over the ownership to sons Herbert, Ralph, and Joseph, and the paper did enjoy some success under executive editor Herbert Swope. One new *World* creation was the first crossword puzzle published in a newspaper in December 1913. It also produced the first *World Almanac*, an annual book recounting events from the previous year and thousands of other facts.

In 1931, Pulitzer's three sons sold the paper for $5 million to Roy Howard, who represented the Scripps-Howard newspaper chain. Howard immediately shut down the *World*, laying off 3,000 workers in the process. The final issue of the *World* was published on February 27, 1931.

Howard merged the *World* name with a Scripps-Howard afternoon paper, the *Evening Telegram*. The *World-Telegram and Sun*, as it came to be known, was published for 35 years before meeting its end in 1966. It merged with the *New York Herald-Tribune*, but the combined newspapers lasted only one more year before closing.

of McKinley. Most New York newspapers chimed
in with criticism of Hearst. But Pulitzer stressed to
his editors that Hearst and his campaign must be
covered with accuracy and objectivity. However,
the *World* did endorse Charles Evans Hughes, to
whom Hearst lost the election.

Losing Control

Meanwhile, Pulitzer was becoming angrier and
more difficult to please. He showed signs of paranoia
and suspicion. In 1907, Kate pleaded with him to
allow her to join him in Europe. He turned her
down but then accused her of abandoning him. That
prompted his wife to write him a letter that expressed
her concerns about his mental state:

> *You refused to let me or me & the children join you. . . .
> You then cable that it is a reflection on the family that
> they are not with you, all this worries me greatly & makes
> me extremely anxious as to your nervous, as well as physical
> condition. . . . If you knew how miserable I feel about you,
> how many wakeful nights I spend thinking of you, you
> would give me more definite information & more frequent.
> . . . You would be so much happier my dear Joseph if you
> would only believe in the friendly intentions & good feeling of
> the people around you.*[3]

It was too late for Pulitzer to change. But he did find a new joy in his last years from his specially made yacht. The 304-foot (93-m) vessel he named *Liberty* was one of the largest private boats in the world. It could travel 6,000 miles (9,656 km) without refueling. The thick doors ensured quiet. His room featured an expansive library from which he could choose books to be read to him.

Pulitzer raved about the yacht to secretary Arthur H. Billing. He spoke about the peace of mind it gave him. When sailing on the *Liberty*, Pulitzer no longer lived in fear. As he told Billing:

> *I love this boat. Here I am at home and comfortable. In a house I am lost in my blindness, always fearful of falling on stairs or obstacles. Here the narrow [corridors] give me safe guidance and I can find my way about alone. Nothing in all my life has given me so much pleasure.* [4]

Quite a Tribute

Among the most eloquent tributes to Pulitzer after his death was uttered by *Boston Globe* editor Charles H. Taylor, who called the publishing great, "one of the giants of journalism, not only of this country but of the world. His career was one of the most brilliant, inspiring, and successful that has ever been known in the journalism of the world. . . . Though a strong Democrat, he criticized his own party as savagely as he did the opposition. He reported Republican conventions and meetings as fully and as impartially as he did those of the Democrats." [5]

A 1962 photo of Joseph Pulitzer III, grandson of Joseph Pulitzer, and editor and publisher of the St. Louis Post-Dispatch *for 38 years*

CHARGES OF LIBEL

In 1908, President Theodore Roosevelt filed a libel lawsuit against Pulitzer. The *World* had printed a story claiming that Roosevelt had helped his fellow Republicans profit from a deal revolving around the construction of the Panama Canal.

The article accused Roosevelt of lying about the secret deals, which motivated Roosevelt to take Pulitzer to court. However, Pulitzer spent the winter sailing in the Atlantic Ocean, outside the three-mile (4.8-km) limit of the United States.

On February 17, 1909, the court indicted Pulitzer and his editors for libel, but the staff at the *World* refused to be intimidated. *World* Editor Frank Cobb made that clear when he wrote,

> Mr. Roosevelt is an episode. The World is an institution. Long after Mr. Roosevelt is dead, long after Mr. Pulitzer is dead, long after all the present editors of this paper are dead, The World will still go on as a great independent newspaper, unmuzzled, undaunted and unterrorized.[6]

By this time, President William Howard Taft had taken office. The charges against Pulitzer were dismissed on January 10, 1910.

THE FINAL DAY

On October 29, 1911, Pulitzer summoned a secretary to read to him on his beloved yacht that was harbored off the coast of Charleston, South Carolina. But as he listened, he began to feel intense pain. Soon, Kate and son Herbert were by his bedside. By early afternoon, assistant Jabez Dunningham, with tears running down his cheeks, told the crew that Pulitzer was dying.

Indeed, the *Liberty*'s flag was soon flying at half-mast. Sixty-four-year-old Joseph Pulitzer died of heart failure. More than 600 people attended his funeral, and more gathered outside. William Randolph Hearst, his rival, spoke glowingly about the contribution Pulitzer had made to journalism. He wrote,

A towering figure in National and International journalism has passed away; a mighty democratic force in the life of this Nation and in the activity of the world has ceased; a great power uniformly exerted in behalf of popular rights and human progress has ended. Joseph Pulitzer is dead. . . . Not the great success which Joseph Pulitzer achieved nor the great wealth which he accumulated nor his association with men of selfish purposes and class prejudices, ever deprived him of his essential democracy or calloused him to the requirements of the democratic masses.

Together at the End

Wife Kate barely arrived in time to be by Joseph's side when he died. She received a telegraph stating that her husband was sick. She had read such notes before, but she felt a premonition that this one could mark the end of Joseph's life. That feeling grew when she arrived at 1:20 p.m. and found Joseph unconscious. He died so quietly and gently that Kate did not know that he had passed away.

Pulitzer Prizes

Pulitzer's 1904 will provided for the creation of the Pulitzer Prizes, administered by an advisory board. Pulitzer originally established awards for journalism, letters, education, and four traveling scholarships. In letters, awards were given for an American novel, an original play performed in New York, a book on the history of the United States, an American biography, and a history of public service by the press. However, he gave the advisory board power to change the number and type of awards as it saw fit. Today, 21 awards are offered each year. Since its creation, the board has added categories for poetry, music, and photography.

The cause of the people Joseph Pulitzer and his newspapers ever espoused ably and intelligently, sympathetically and powerfully. In his death journalism has lost a leader, the people a champion, the Nation a valuable citizen.[7]

A LEGACY

Pulitzer's legacy lives on through his influence on journalism and on the world. It also grows through the Graduate School of Journalism at Columbia University, which he founded, and the awards that bear his name. The first Pulitzer Prizes for journalism were presented in 1917 and remain an annual honor presented to those who reach the highest standards in the profession—the standards set by Hungarian immigrant Joseph Pulitzer.

Joseph Pulitzer

TIMELINE

1847	1853	1864
Joseph Pulitzer is born to Philip and Louise in Mako, Hungary, on April 10.	The Pulitzer family moves to Budapest.	Pulitzer applies with the Austrian, French, and British military but is turned down.

1867	1868	1869
Pulitzer becomes a U.S. citizen.	Pulitzer lands a job as a reporter for the *Westliche Post* in St. Louis.	Pulitzer is elected as Missouri state representative on December 21.

1864	**1865**	**1865**
Pulitzer agrees to fight with the Union Army in the American Civil War.	Pulitzer begins looking for work in New York City.	Pulitzer hops aboard a train as a stowaway and goes to live in St. Louis, Missouri.

1876	**1877**	**1878**
Pulitzer meets future wife Kate Davis while working as a *New York Sun* correspondent.	Pulitzer survives a deadly hotel fire in St. Louis, Missouri, on April 10.	Pulitzer marries Kate Davis on June 19.

TIMELINE

1878	1883	1884
Pulitzer purchases what becomes known as the *St. Louis Post-Dispatch*.	Pulitzer purchases the *New York World* from Jay Gould on May 9.	Pulitzer wins a congressional seat in November but resigns four months later.

1896	1898	1910
The era of yellow journalism begins as Pulitzer's *World* competes with Hearst's *New York Journal*.	In November, Pulitzer returns the *World* to its former policy of truth and accuracy in reporting.	Pulitzer survives a lawsuit filed against him by President Theodore Roosevelt.

1887	**1890**	**1890**
Pulitzer claims that the *World* is the most read newspaper in the world.	Pulitzer withdraws as editor of the *World* on October 16.	The *World* moves into the tallest building in the United States on December 10.

1911	**1912**	**1917**
On October 29, Pulitzer dies on his yacht near Charleston, South Carolina.	The Columbia School of Journalism is officially opened.	The first Pulitzer Prizes are awarded.

Essential Facts

Date of Birth

April 10, 1847

Place of Birth

Mako, Hungary

Date of Death

October 29, 1911

Parents

Philip and Louise Pulitzer

Education

Pulitzer was tutored at home and attended private schools in Hungary.

Marriage

Kate Davis (June 19, 1878)

Children

Ralph, Lucille, Katherine, Joseph Jr., Edith, Constance, Herbert

CAREER HIGHLIGHTS

❖ Pulitzer purchased what became the *St. Louis Post-Dispatch* in 1878. As his paper's coverage focused on exposing immorality, circulation soared until the paper was consumed by scandal.

❖ Pulitzer took ownership of the *New York World* in 1883, bringing a crusading style of journalism to the newspaper. Coverage mixed sensational stories with in-depth stories on serious issues.

❖ In 1887, Pulitzer claimed the *New York World* was the most read newspaper on Earth, with a daily circulation topping 300,000.

SOCIETAL CONTRIBUTIONS

❖ Pulitzer is credited with creating a new style of journalism and with setting standards for fairness and accuracy that have influenced newspapers since.

❖ Pulitzer left an endowment of $2 million to create the Columbia School of Journalism and $2 million to establish the Pulitzer Prizes.

CONFLICTS

❖ Amid a circulation battle with the *New York Journal*, the *World* temporarily engaged in a period of yellow journalism before returning to its commitment to accuracy.

❖ In 1908, President Theodore Roosevelt accused Pulitzer and the *World* of libel.

QUOTE

"The highest satisfaction felt by the director of the *World* in its success comes from the reflection that it has not been won by any sacrifice of principle, any surrender of conviction, any appeal to party spirit or class prejudice."—*Joseph Pulitzer*

ADDITIONAL RESOURCES

SELECT BIBLIOGRAPHY

Barrett, James Wyman. *Joseph Pulitzer and His* World. New York: Vanguard, 1941.

Pfaff, Daniel W. *Joseph Pulitzer II and the* Post-Dispatch: *A Newspaperman's Life*. University Park, PA: Pennsylvania State UP, 1991.

Seitz, Don Carlos. *Joseph Pulitzer: His Life and Letters,* New York: AMS, 1970.

Swanberg, W. A. *Pulitzer*. New York: Charles Scribner's Sons, 1967.

FURTHER READING

Cohen, Daniel. *Yellow Journalism: Scandal, Sensationalism and Gossip in the Media.* Breckenridge, CO: Twenty-First Century, 2000.

Whitelaw, Nancy. *Joseph Pulitzer and the* New York World. Greensboro, NC: Morgan Reynolds, 2000.

Web Links

To learn more about Joseph Pulitzer, visit ABDO Publishing Company online at **www.abdopublishing.com**. Web sites about Joseph Pulitzer are featured on our Book Links page. These links are routinely monitored and updated to provide the most current information available.

Places to Visit

The Journalism School at Columbia University
2950 Broadway, New York, NY 10027
www.journalism.columbia.edu
This journalism school was founded with an endowment left by Joseph Pulitzer. The board administering the Pulitzer Prizes is housed there.

Newseum
555 Pennsylvania Ave. NW, Washington, DC 20001
888-639-7386
www.newseum.org
This interactive museum features exhibits covering five centuries of news history, including a gallery of Pulitzer Prize-winning photographs.

GLOSSARY

anti-Semitism
Prejudice against and persecution of Jewish people.

circulation
The number of newspapers sold during a particular period of time.

Confederacy
The Southern states that seceded from the United States and fought to form their own nation during the American Civil War.

Congress
The national legislative body of the United States consisting of the Senate and the House of Representatives.

corruption
Any form of illegal activity done by those entrusted by the public in an attempt to create personal gain.

crusade
Any campaign or movement to improve a situation.

editor
A person responsible for the content that goes into a newspaper or other written publication.

editorial
An article published by a newspaper that states the opinion of an editor or other writer.

immigrant
An individual who has moved from another country.

indicted
Charged with a crime.

journalism
The profession consisting of all jobs within the newspaper, magazine, or electronic news media businesses.

legislature
A political body that can change or create laws.

libel
> The publication of untrue, unfair statements that are damaging to someone's reputation.

Magyar
> The people who settled Hungary in the ninth century.

paranoia
> The unwarranted belief by an individual that others are planning to harm him or her in some way.

publisher
> An individual who runs the business side of a newspaper or a magazine, generally its owner.

sensationalism
> The practice of exaggerating the importance of news stories in an attempt to increase circulation.

Union
> The Northern army during the American Civil War that fought to keep the United States together.

yellow journalism
> A term used to describe the practice of sensationalism in U.S. journalism during the late nineteenth and early twentieth centuries.

Source Notes

Chapter 1. Birth of a Journalist
1. Don Carlos Seitz. *Joseph Pulitzer: His Life and Letters*. New York: Simon & Schuster, 1924. 51.
2. Denis Brian. *Pulitzer: A Life*. New York: Wiley, 2001. 11.
3. W. A. Swanberg. *Pulitzer*. New York: Scribner's Sons, 1967. 8.

Chapter 2. In Hungary, Hungry to Fight
None.

Chapter 3. First Taunted, Then Embraced
1. Denis Brian. *Pulitzer: A Life*. New York: Wiley, 2001. 44.
2. W. A. Swanberg. *Pulitzer*. New York: Scribner's Sons, 1967. 10.
3. Denis Brian. *Pulitzer: A Life*. New York: Wiley, 2001. 14.
4. "A Great Hotel Burned." *New York Times*, 12 Apr. 1877: 1. NYTimes.com. 29 Mar. 2009 <http://query.nytimes.com/mem/archive-free/pdf?res=9A01E4D7103AE63BBC4A52DFB266838C669FDE>.

Chapter 4. Marriage, Fame, and Fortune

1. Don Carlos Seitz. *Joseph Pulitzer: His Life and Letters*, New York: Simon & Schuster, 1924. 91–92.

2. "Joseph Pulitzer Dies Suddenly." *New York Times*, 30 Oct. 1911. 8 Mar. 2009 <http://query.nytimes.com/gst/abstract.html?res=950 0E5DE1231E233A25753C3A9669D946096D6CF>.

3. Denis Brian. *Pulitzer: A Life*. New York: Wiley, 2001. 33.

Chapter 5. Taking Over the *World*

1. Maury Klein. *The Life and Legend of Jay Gould*. Baltimore, MD: Johns Hopkins UP, 1997. 2.

2. Frank Luther Mott. *American Journalism*. New York: Macmillan, 1941. 436. Google Book Search. 8 Mar. 2009 <http://books. google.com/books?id=3TyVKPLyWOwC&dq=american+journalis m+frank+luther+mott&printsec=frontcover&source=bl&ots=j0Iakg 0lfb&sig=paDXcVEGjvLnhM11n5kizGvWByE&hl=en&ei=Af6zScq- Bo6-M8fQqMUE&sa=X&oi=book_result&resnum=1&ct=result#PP A9,M1>.

3. W. A. Swanberg. *Pulitzer*. New York: Scribner's Sons, 1967. 70.

4. James B. Townsend. "The Many-Sided Pulitzer, by One Who Knew Him." *New York Times*, 5 Nov. 1911. 13 Apr. 2009 <http:// query.nytimes.com/gst/abstract.html?res=9D06EEDF1E31E233A2 5756C0A9679D946096D6CF>.

Source Notes Continued

Chapter 6. New Ideas Pay Off
1. W.A. Swanberg. *Pulitzer*. New York: Scribner's Sons, 1967. 104.

Chapter 7. Acts of Desperation
1. Denis Brian. *Pulitzer: A Life*. New York: Wiley, 2001. 149.
2. James Wyman Barrett. *Joseph Pulitzer and His* World. New York: Vanguard, 1941. 137.
3. Denis Brian. *Pulitzer: A Life*. New York: Wiley, 2001. 162–163.
4. Ibid. 206.
5. Daniel W. Pfaff. *Joseph Pulitzer II and the* Post-Dispatch: *A Newspaperman's Life*. University Park: Pennsylvania State UP, 1991. 26.

Chapter 8. Shame, Spain and the *Maine*
1. Denis Brian. *Pulitzer: A Life*. New York: Wiley, 2001. 191–192.
2. Don Carlos Seitz. *Joseph Pulitzer: His Life and Letters*, New York: Simon & Schuster, 1924. 207.
3. W. A. Swanberg. *Pulitzer*. New York: Scribner's Sons, 1967. 254–255.

Chapter 9. Back to Truth and Accuracy
1. W. A. Swanberg. *Pulitzer*. New York: Scribner's Sons, 1967. 281.
2. Daniel W. Pfaff. *Joseph Pulitzer II and the* Post-Dispatch: *A Newspaperman's Life*. University Par, PA: Pennsylvania State UP, 1991. 33–34.
3. W. A. Swanberg. *Pulitzer*. New York: Scribner's Sons, 1967. 283.
4. Denis Brian. *Pulitzer: A Life*. New York: Wiley, 2001. 284.
5. Ibid.

Chapter 10. Death of a Publishing Giant
1. "Joseph Pulitzer Dies Suddenly." *New York Times*, 30 Oct. 1911: 1. 25 Mar. 2009 <http://query.nytimes.com/gst/abstract.html?res=9 500E5DE1231E233A25753C3A9669D946096D6CF>.
2. Denis Brian. *Pulitzer: A Life*. New York: Wiley, 2001. 292.
3. W. A. Swanberg. *Pulitzer*. New York: Scribner's Sons, 1967. 337.
4. Don Carlos Seitz. *Joseph Pulitzer: His Life and Letters*, New York: Simon & Schuster, 1924. 290.
5. Denis Brian. *Pulitzer: A Life*. New York: Wiley, 2001. 389.
6. W. A. Swanberg. *Pulitzer*. New York: Scribner's Sons, 1967. 371.
7. William Randolph Hearst. "Praise of Pulitzer as a Journalist." *New York Times*. 30.Oct. 1911: 2. 25 Mar. 2009 <http://query. nytimes.com/mem/archive-free/pdf?_r=1&res=9D03E5DE1231E2 33A25753C3A9669D946096D6CF>.

INDEX

ABOUT THE AUTHOR

Martin Gitlin is a freelance writer based in northeast Ohio. He won more than 40 awards as a newspaper reporter, including first place for general excellence from Associated Press in 1995. That organization also selected him as one of the top four feature writers in the state in 2001. Gitlin has written more than a dozen educational books, including historical works on *Brown v. Board of Education*, the Battle of the Little Bighorn, the 1929 stock market crash, and Operation Desert Storm, as well as biographies on Princess Diana and Audrey Hepburn.

PHOTO CREDITS